NATURAL HISTORY
& OTHER POEMS

Dan Chiasson was born in Burlington, Vermont, and educated at Amherst College and Harvard University, where he completed a PhD in English. A widely published literary critic, Chiasson is the author of *One Kind of Everything: Poem and Person in Contemporary America* (University of Chicago Press, 2006). He has published two poetry collections in the States, *The Afterlife of Objects* (University of Chicago Press, 2002) and *Natural History* (Knopf, 2005). *Natural History & other poems* (Bloodaxe Books, 2006), combining work from both his US collections with later work, is his first British publication.

He has received a Pushcart Prize and a Whiting Writers' Award, and teaches at Wellesley College. He lives in Sherborn, Massachusetts.

DAN CHIASSON

Natural History

& OTHER POEMS

BLOODAXE BOOKS

ISBN: 1 85224 736 3

First published 2006 by
Bloodaxe Books Ltd,
Highgreen,
Tarset,
Northumberland NE48 1RP.

www.bloodaxebooks.com
For further information about Bloodaxe titles
please visit our website or write to
the above address for a catalogue.

Bloodaxe Books Ltd acknowledges
the financial assistance of
Arts Council England, North East.

Cover printing by J. Thomson Colour Printers Ltd, Glasgow.

Printed in Great Britain by
Bell & Bain Limited, Glasgow.

ACKNOWLEDGEMENTS

This book consists of a selection of poems from *The Afterlife of Objects* (University of Chicago Press, 2002), the entire text of *Natural History* (Alfred A. Knopf, 2005), with the addition of nine new, previously uncollected poems. Special thanks are due to the University of Chicago Press and Alfred A. Knopf (a division of Random House, Inc) for their help in facilitating the publication of this book, and in particular to editors Randy Petilos and Deborah Garrison respectively.

Acknowledgements are due to the editors of the following publications in which some of the new poems first appeared: *The New Yorker* ('Little Boy', 'Mosaic of a Hare, Corinium, 100 AD'), *The Paris Review* ('Here Follows an Account of the Nature of Birds', 'A Posy') and *Ploughshares* ('Etruscan Song').

CONTENTS

NATURAL HISTORY (2005)

from

THE AFTERLIFE OF OBJECTS

(2002)

In reflecting on the *modus operandi* of our consciousness of time, we are at first tempted to suppose it the easiest thing in the world to understand. Our inner states succeed each other. They know themselves as they are; then of course, we say, they must know their own succession. But this philosophy is too crude: for between the mind's own changes *being* successive and *knowing their own succession*, lies as broad a chasm as between the object and subject of any case of cognition in the world. *A succession of feelings, in and of itself is not a feeling of succession. And since, to our succession of feelings, a feeling of their succession is added, that must be treated as an additional fact requiring its own special elucidation.*

WILLIAM JAMES,
Principles of Psychology

We cannot fall out of this world.

CHRISTIAN DIETRICH GRABBE,
Hannibal

I

Nocturne

Do our words count so late at night,
this late do even these words count?

In life I was heroic at times, at
other times quiet as a mug of milk.

I saved a man I swear, but afterward
wherever I walked I saw one drown.

Men cry their names out when they die
and one man as he died cried *Dan*.

Back then I thought the water was air;
I thought the body was a bar of soap.

Other and Other made a ladder and up
to the top I climbed and saw America.

Other and Other made a mirror and in
I stepped and watched the water heal.

Of course there was no *man* no *Dan*,
I'm speaking in terms of the moon –

and anyway this late at night our words
can't count. Not even these words count.

Your Stone

Here's your stone he said *what for* I said *for your girl* he said
and left me alone in the bedroom strewn with punctured cans.

They bring the fire so close to their face I thought every time
the living-room flashed and wild cries climbed to ecstatic silence.

Ecstatic silence: just yesterday alone in my study I heard
the neighbor's child practicing scales on a rented clarinet

just last night when your crying ended and you fell asleep
I prayed to be made inanimate, a hand-me-down mattress.

But tonight the little crystal called forgetfulness, the postures
of delight and appetite, and the beautiful girl said *what's your name?*

Vermont

I was the west
once. I was paradise.

My beauty ruined me: the old
excuse. Perhaps

if I was rich, remote
or fine – but paradise

is always just
too close, too coarse.

Men made me;
though in memory they seem
more steel than

flesh, more copper
than intelligence or whim, ambition, will –

what makes men, anyway? Always
groaning on the far end

of some lever, sharpening some blade.

If I were farther, Jupiter
or Babylon, the ocean
bottom, I

might have been a story. Stories never ruined anybody.

But paradise is always only
close enough, just

west, the next, the next, the sun
halved every evening on the same line of

the poem, the poem itself

a minute in the history of minutes. Then
decorative and north,
unstoried, white. And after that, pure

thoroughfare. My signs are written twice.

'The Sensible Present Has Duration'

O blistering cabinet

*

O mahogany, O birch pipes,
pipe rack, hardcover

books – *The Last Convertible*, *Trinity*,
The Royal Wedding,

biography of Patton.
Railroad spike inscribed

On your thirtieth year as
a soldier, from the 73rd.

Mail-order crest, name etched
in "runic" script.

O photograph

*

swollen
by false cures, my uncle

age nine, no more
appointments, strawberry-sized

tumors dotting his spine,
O icicle, formed for dissolution,

"pride" or portent. Military olive.
Toque, wool surrogate.

He stands beside a sapling
lilac, white twin, blossoming.

O window

*

Outside, my grandfather wheeling
a pesticide tank

from tree to tree, spraying everything
with thick, white foam –

bark, leaf, apple flesh –
salting the garden

with handfuls of red sand, dissolving
aphid, Japanese beetle, horned tomato worm

as thick as rope. Gone
in an instant, emerging

from his fiberglass outbuilding shed, helving
an axe, bright blade, pine handle,

to eliminate
a dwarf peach weakened by nesting beetles.

O ordinary axe

*

lilac, uncle, window, cabinet
lost, not lost, mere home

I merely left, look away
made elegy: a book's

fifth edition, its
yellow cover, not the available red,

instruction manual
for an old-world

Beta VCR, *The Way*
split by a nylon dividing-ribbon.

                                        *

An out-of-print book.

A remainder.

Boston

When it was time to pass outside myself I sought
the nearest
famous city, nearest

place whose boundaries were not contiguous with mine –

downstate, wax autumn sprayed
with the dust of the pulverised hillside, miles

of it dynamited and all
I-89 made
rabbit warren and collapsing domino.

Inside
the famous city, no one knew me, everyone

walked carrying books
called *Tintoretto*, *Giotto* –

frescoes set
by the blaring of an

ambulance, a man miming

his mother's lullabies, a lady
purring *Rattlesnake O Rattlesnake*

to calm her spastic arm. Ahead,

the 'horrific glazed
perpendiculars of the future' –

and once I saw a man trying
to steady an
aquarium on his bent knee, nearly

impossible to carry,
lose his

grip and fish and glass were everywhere.

'The Anatomy of Melancholy'
(for D.T.)

I

You turned the lights out to read 'Lycidas' holding the very berries
'harsh and crude' Milton held reluctantly for his school friend.

Then memory, imprecise but more precise than mine, went rummaging
for ivy and laurel, laurel and myrtle, all the tangled syntax candor

still takes to be revealed, even between two friends. Later, you dreamed
the whole poem came unspooled and lay tangled around your feet.

II

Or is Burton's *Anatomy* your model, making sadness
excess and excess precision, piles of the stuff.

Burton, who blackened his forearms with melancholy ink?
One time we tried crushing our Zoloft up and doing lines

of it, but you were right, or Burton was: it 'misaffected' us
and made us 'bursten-bellied, writhren and blear-eyed'.

III

Your dissertation pictured seventeenth-century men picturing grief,
that ocean bottom dark but for occasional punk-rock

coral and ghoulish man-o-wars that hover over it.
You followed Milton following his school friend down

the monstrous deep to find a likeness of your own sad mind,
a coral ruler with a coral scepter sitting on a coral throne.

Paul 1:13

When I became a man my childish things
began to pile up
and putrefy. They were like heirlooms, other people's

things trying to mean *my past*
inside the gilt
upholstered future they arranged for me.

I feared them years before the forklift
came and dumped
them in the living-room.

Now it is night, and all I am
is souvenirs of youth:
toy hammer, donkey's ass, and cancer ward.

Dactyls after Driving through Nevada
(for J.P.)

If at a party a stranger approaches,
      friend of a friend or cousin from home
O how will I greet him? Crisscrossing

Nevada, highwayside shrines
      write *wreck* in italics: one
pilgrimage done, another begun.

What was it you said about
      guardrails, their miles and
miles of comical silence? Or road signs,

so weird in the ultimate landscape –
      the nothingness named; or what
seems to be nothingness, canyon and

trace, evergreen grove, the rivers with
      Spanish and Indian names –
and what if that friend of a friend had a

brother returning from Europe now
      ten years ago, a brother half
hero, half slacker, merely desires and

lovely pretensions (the *Gauloises*
      and Sartre in his carry-on
bag) turned into myth over

Lockerbie, Scotland, spasm and
      flash, suddenly any boy falling alone
through the sky, found in a creamery?

Io

Why must my father's love be written gibberish hieroglyphs
thought a Hawaiian girl named for one of Jupiter's moons

so she moved to Boston to be near the other ocean, the one
that knew not a thing about the unthinkable act or the regime

of compulsory tenderness that followed anon and when she
took me by the hand and said her name was *Io* like the moon

and said *What sort of poems do you write, do you write them
for pretty girls?* I wondered what the hieroglyphs spelled, after all:

did those scared-looking buzzards and lilies and beetles
her father made deep in her heart spell out my name, tonight?

*Once I was a picked flower and my father made my head spin
by rubbing his palms together* said Io, a Hawaiian girl, to me.

Song for a Play

The grief of little boys will make
them monsters, O,
but winter isn't here, hello.

The grief of little girls will make
them sad and sexy.
They'll dress themselves to be

undressed. They'll have an accident, no no.
The mad mothers, hello.
They all name cats after their long

dead brothers, but that isn't winter.
Winter has a long beard
and a hundred petty quarrels.

The suave fathers are leaving, O. They're leaving
but they wave. They wave
but let their watches stop. They like

the drama of the last tick as the spring
goes slack. Time
is their mausoleum.

The sad old men. When
the world forgets them
they read paperbacks and straighten up.

The ladies with the catheters and
bath benches are here
but winter, O, not winter, no.

But then the snow falls down
the yellow bus stops short
and skids, a tin accordion

there's one voyeur for every
widow's window
and it's winter, O, it's here, hello.

'The Glass Slipper'

In the blue light by the bathroom door, near the pay telephones, where
a weird staircase carpeted in red velour leads seemingly nowhere

a Scot is yelling *I'm A Scot* at a terrified dancer yelling back *I'm not*
and suddenly a bouncer carts him away, away; there I am standing

waiting for Mike to make his nightly rounds, astonishing Mike
with a dolphin for loneliness a dolphin for sadness a dolphin for fear

a hundred dolphins in harness drive his chariot and once a night
they appear before you and they're kind, they eat out of your hand.

In my dream I'm Audubon: with an ink for the belly of every bird.
I'm Audubon: with an ink for the injured bird I carry around inside.

In the blue light by the bathroom door, near the pay telephones, there
I wait for Mike to materialise, bold man, those smiling dolphins.

Self

Found not founded. Attacking only
from the back
like the Bengal tiger; afraid

of the face. Sweet-talking like the addict
coveting
another addict's stash. Fished from

my own trash like the feared
letter I heard later
held a birthday check.

Watched like the tiger from
a great height,
hollered out. Two-faced, masked

like the villager tricking
the tiger. Tricked
like the tiger. Founded on owned ground.

II

My Ravine

How will you know what my poem is like
    until you've gone down my ravine and seen

the box springs, mattresses bookcases, and desks
    the neighboring women's college dumps each year,

somebody's hairdryer, someone's Herodotus
    a poem's dream landscape, one-half Latinate and

one-half shit, the neighboring women's college's shit?
    Wheelbarrow upon wheelbarrow a humpbacked

custodian hauls old dormitory furniture down
    and launches it watching it roll into the pile.

You won't know how my poem decides what's in,
    what's out, what decorum means and doesn't mean,

until you follow him home after work and see him
    going wild all night imagining those girls' old beds.

You won't know what I'm trying for until you hear
    how every fall in my backyard a swarm of deer

materialises, scavenging where the raspberries touched
    the radishes, now ploughed under, itching the lawn

for dandelions, stare at each other and wander
    bewildered down my ravine and turn into skeletons.

Poem

When I picture *1940* everyone poses
for me, as though I had the one

camera in the world. I cannot distract them from
their studied, ghoulish jolliness.

My grandmother is posing, yelling
Smile and my grandfather is horsing around

with a tire, making his biceps big. I
can't know the past, because the past

keeps arranging itself before my lens. People call
out *Here* and *Over here*, striking

their prewar, rural, easygoing stances.
That night, when I try again, everyone

is indoors, in parlors, reading quietly.
A woman rocking in and out of lamplight

studies me. The neighbor's
middle child died this afternoon.

Ward

I came quietly where
my grandmother
was an insect

in an iron hive.
No drop
of water fell

more quietly than I
fell through
the elevator shaft.

Then, on the ward,
I walked along
a hallway of formaldehyde

and glass.
A woman bent
herself in half

to scratch her coal-
black swollen foot.
Christ, one man's

forehead shone
white and dewy, like
a dolphin's belly.

Maiden never was who heard
the cribs fall
silent where her daughters were,

whose husband, frozen
still, berated her
one long year from

a piss-soaked chair.
What is awareness
here, so late, so close to night?

'...and yet the end must be as 'tis'

Soon, the laminated

tag, her name formed
in tangling lilies –

the t-shirts,
sweatshirts, robes

bought to replace
her old, coarse clothes,

the photographs this time
taken from the album, this time

held (crumbling, sciliate
with adhesive)

then the machine called

what: *Elysium?*
what: *halcyon?*

slumber, health, the old life,
memory –?

the truth
that underneath
her terry cloth

jersey is her body
unscarred, relieved

of her lost sons, as

she is helped into
a bath, her body

white, softening like an acorn

in a cup
of water – then "covered", clean

beneath
the kitsch
of death.

Visit

(Latin, 'he saw', 'he viewed')

Dying was not a change
of clothes, not a chance

to wear pajamas. I knew
his limbs were stiffening

for seven years, like one
of Dante's suicides kept

alive inside a tree. He knew
each ache would harden

him at last, he watched
it happen to himself, and

watched me watching him.
He saw me from his window

take a fly rod from
his shed and put it in my car.

He said 'I saw you steal
my trout rod,' which meant

'I haven't died.' So I
returned it. Seeing him

die was like seeing a boy
inflate a sandwich bag

with breath, then empty it.
His flesh that had been

flesh, then Elm, was Ash.
I stayed a week, and

when he wasn't dying
anymore, I went away.

Anonymous Bust of a Man, *c.* AD 100 (Cyprus)

It is hard
to remember about the hardening man

he is alive, hard not
to hear

in the shrill nonsense

he speaks when he attempts to speak
the chirping

of a thrush, any
ordinary bird

hard to see
(but look) beneath

his sagging mask a face, once
flesh, now

lost, a planet –
barren and featureless as Pluto.

His eyes are not
two animals

playing tired, only
to pounce once

we pass by – he is no oak
to kiss beside.

His head twists on its stem.

Deer

My mother wishes
for a ghost's life.

She wants her dress to blow
against itself, not

against her skin, she asks
to be all breath, mind, gauze,

she hates the calcified *events*
composing her –

births, deaths, the old plateaus.

But when she begs
to lose all flesh she sees

her father's back bent
over a doe

he shot that morning, cleaning
her in our backyard.

He trims the bone of muscle,
gristle. Far off, he seems

to pray above her, or
to grieve, like Cephalus for his young wife;

but he is not grieving.

Evening, dinner, my grandmother
calling him inside. He takes

the hide intact into
his shed, hanging it to dry

like a woman's soaked gown.

One

The hour since midnight
was so full of me. The next hour will be better.

I will read Horace in
the quietest translation. I'll drink the water

in my water glass,
no more, no less.

The metaphors I'll use will be
those walking
humbly in the world already, foxes

without anything
to fear, the glow
of moonlight in their fur,

white grass before the other colors ripen.

Though she ransacked
my innocence,
transformed my house from silence

to the low gargle of sickness
and old age,
the night nurse with her pile of

crosswords on the cot, to her

the cot and crosswords,
night nurse
and formica table top were beautiful, almost a meadow.

I will do nothing more to night tonight.

III

Cicada

I

The 'lily-like' cry from the tops
      of olive trees, or in my childhood

from maple trees that lined the road
      down to the beach: is it the call

of men held inside bodies so small
      they might have held them in their palms

once, when they were whole, who now
      are brittle and wail from treetops?

Forgetful of their bodies, these
      men housed themselves in music

when music like a new color
      declared itself on earth. Imagine

the silence before music, all
      the open mouths with no notes

coming out, like the mouths in paintings,
      underwater mouths, agape, the way

we picture suffering. It was
      like coming up for air when music

appeared here, and these men starved
      themselves for fear eating might stop

the beauty up. *Mousomania*,
      'music-madness'; and so the gods pitied

these men and pitying made them sing
      O let me sing you past this night.

II

And so the night I came home late
     and found one skating on my bedroom

mirror I was terrified, both for
     the poor soul trapped inside the green

contraption like a child fallen down
     a well, and for myself, forced to choose

whether to handle or to house
     the brittle man. I hate provoking

wildness in things – the strange dog's eyes
     met inadvertently, the housefly held

electric between panes; as a child
     I was so scared of my friends' fathers

I would hide when they got home from work.
     So all that night in bed I lay

awake, afraid at any moment the cicada
     might start crying as he did

perched on Eunomos's bow the time
     the fifth string broke, when

from an olive tree he dropped and
     landed where the slack string hung

and sang Eunomos's instrument
     'whole again and wholly beautiful'.

III

Two people lie awake together
in one bed. They do not speak.

Each knows the other is awake
and knows the other knows.

Why can't they speak? As though
    a spell held them in place or some

god's architecture fastened
    their helpless limbs together –

as though their tongues were thick
    as loaves of bread inside their throats.

But this is love, each wants the other
    to escape the ceremonies of day,

each makes the night a little fantasy
    of night, a warm home decked with sleep.

Night after night they lie this way,
    no sleep, no speech, until one night

the telephone erupts and they sit up
    till dawn together, rocked by grief.

   IV

The night I came home late and on
    my bedroom mirror saw that child

I imagined my own child: far
    from me because as yet unmade,

apart because imaginary, but the best
    boy there, the prettiest in that kingdom.

Baffled, he watches me as I assemble
    doctrine and dog shit, the junk

of adult life I learned watching TV.
    He gets to learn by watching me

pretend he's not alive, a lesson
    in resemblance and absence,

skill, refusal, all the usual lies
        you parse and press yourself against.

He gets to see me blank out slowly,
        the TV left on past the programming.

His mother will gradually grow to fear
        him there, in that vague place

since as he changes to my twin
        he changes to her enemy, the boy turned

to the man, the man uncannily
        like the father he could never know.

   IV

Sometimes this song feels like a cure
        sometimes it makes the hurt much worse.

But it's the most brilliant defense —
        no judge ever lacked sympathy for this,

I'm making it up as I go along,
        but people like to think it's fate.

And so the night I came home late
        the actual cicada on my real mirror

scared me, for I hate handling anything
        I know needs my help fathoming

this maze of chairs and bottles and books,
        the mess I make of any room with my

unruly inwardness. Of course
        I couldn't kill it, where would I hide

the awful handful afterwards?
        That night I knew old men lie

awake the night they start to die;
        the room is solemn, full of something

they can't scare away,
        their souls, or childhood fears

they never solved, that stick to them
        like burrs or barnacles.

Their parents reappear at their bedside
        miming the ancient attitudes of

tenderness and rue, adoring them –
        and like the figures on a frieze

all those they loved appear as they were
        but mute, their eyes and lips sewn shut.

Then from inside the room a cry;
        and then the cicada flies away.

Stealing from Your Mother

I

Knowing her schedule you're half
way there. Watch the house dim and become

a museum; then

the familiar door, familiar
corridor, familiar
drawer. You know

the heirlooms from the junk.

You saw her cooing attachments form
over the years; now

you know where her best stuff is.

Her ring. Her wedding china.
The cameo of her grandmother.

Those are *pearls* that were
her pearls, and she

is somewhere else now, Florida
or on an errand; you know
several escapes.

There, in her closet, under
columns

of forgotten dresses, the sheer

dry-cleaner's plastic like a second skin –

Reward. Now it never wasn't yours.

II

The poem takes on a conscience. You wish
for your old self, unscrupulous,

pissed. You aren't exceptional.
Your wife wears pearls. Your real house

is a trick of light; the old one, gone,
is real enough to burn. Lacking

conviction, you will spend forever
sentencing yourself You know

what you did. You know you know
what you did. No one is hearing your ornate confession.

Spade

I dreamed I was the spade
my mother used

to dig her marigolds in spring,
her *bloom* and *worry*.

Her digging, throwing, patting to bring
rows to life, each
blooms familiar

to worry, each row perfect, bloom,
rich dirt between, planned
absence and full, superfluous bloom –

I made the trench her hand proposed;

I was the pressure in her palm;

her *ache from planting*
was
my *presence in her life*.

Blueprint

I

I made God, God's
son, the angels and
the clouds of heaven

for my neighbor, an older boy
I loved and
whom I'd angered.

I made the clouds
from the unraveled
tips of cotton swabs.

Heaven was
a shoebox; building
heaven was fair

punishment
for calling him our pet name
within earshot

of his older friends.
Why do I see him, even
now: wild in shame, arms

waving, dangerouis, trying
to erase
that syllable from air?

II

That year
he'd taken me
behind our shed to see

'what men and women do alone'.
I was eight.
It was not his usual

48

locker-room patois.
He stacked
the twenty bleached-and-tattered

magazines atop
a quarter-cord of birch.
A light-blue plastic

tarp slapped
at the pile, keeping
the wood crisp

and combustible. Wax
pages, photographs:
the done-unto under

the doing, subduing
wave after
subduing wave:

girls sitting
still until
things settle.

Fact lost
in the shiny
satin drapery of fascination.

III
The Lord so loved the world
he sent
a steaming pile of

lasagna for
my ninth birthday.
A plate. Another. One

cascading square
waits on
a spatula; our priest

arrives. My mother greets him.
His peck
on my forehead

is full, unwelcome.
He squires me
from relative

to relative
collecting gifts:
sweater, eight-track, monster mask.

Father Tom in ordinary
clothes! I am
a special child.

Later, drunk, cursing
in Latin,
everyone in stitches,

he'll ash
his cigarette
on my bare arm.

IV

Another neighbor, later that same
summer. 'Jamey':
contraband, a troublemaker, stammering

across the fence
at me *Who who
who who's your fa-*

father, fucker? Or
*Fucker doesn't
have a father.*

He'd read his Freud.
He knew
the blueprint of this poem, and others

I will have to write.
Then one
gray ordinary day

his father held him
down and nearly fucked
the life out of him.

Then he was quieter, and I
became sole
ruler of the neighborhood.

Purple Blouse

Then I dreamed I chose
the purple blouse my mother

wore the morning she conceived
me – dressed her, felt her

expectation as my own, her life
now distillate of her one wish

her saying *Yes* to the thing thrown
over her.

Matter

They found her purse in Africa.

*

Her watch was found, still
wound, in Maine; one

of her blouses as
discovered
floating in the Everglades, among

the yawning crocodiles.

The chilly metal eyeglasses I
still can feel
on my forehead, which I

would recognise beside
a hundred other pairs, were chosen from among

a hundred other pairs
by an ironic adolescent in Chicago –

*

matter can neither be created nor
destroyed: but where

is her firm voice outside
my bedroom door, where

is the slow comforting scrape and toss of snow
shoveling in 1981, the neighbor

showing off his blind
granddaughter, my 20/20 vision suddenly

obscene, embarrassing –

＊

Tonight I find her bone
and pewter rosary

coiling on my bedside table.

A Salt Dish
Horace, Odes 2:16

At a table the size of my writing table, Horace's
happy man sits polishing his father's
salt dish, wearing the outer surface out, making it shine.

How small happiness seems, compared say
to the roller-coaster they unveiled in
Florida, its corkscrew tail a football field long.

Today, I watched my friend descend his entryway
stairs in so much pain he seemed to move
through lava, lava pooling and pooling where

his limbs tried to take root, his light feet trying
to be heavy stone, not feather down, and
the fucked eventuality of his body worried every step.

Small meaningful trinkets for the rest of us. Heirlooms.
Something to hold a handful of material, some
vessel where the otherwise always-loosening self will settle.

The Afterlife of Objects

The lilac behind glass, the old hoe brought inside.

> *I dreamed I lay asleep wrapped*
> *in the lilac's stifling embrace.*

> *I woke and found the old hoe in my bed,*
> *my limbs were caked with loam.*

The crumbling mica of old dust-jackets.

> *I dreamed I was covered with the chalk*
> *of flaking pages of military histories.*

> *I woke and found I'd authored*
> *Vermont's evacuation plans.*

The cellar where canned meat was stored.

> *In my dream, the Kennedys invite*
> *me to a picnic, they are just like us.*

> *My grandfather wrote the code*
> *that kept the Cold War hanging there.*

The old hoe brought inside. The fly rod I tried to steal.

> *I thought his eyes were tired*
> *because his arms and legs were tied.*

> *I never wished him dead,*
> *I wished him blind.*

IV

Peach Tree

When did I plant this peach tree in my sleep and why
now does it seem to bloom
as though in answer to a prayer?

I did not ask to see the tree extend its bough so far
it almost disappeared
but finally unfolded this white flower.

I lived so long fearing the world's quaint
insufficiencies were mine –
as air would conjure earth, earth, air

I stared at the little life made in my name, and thanked
the immediate and thanked the near.
I thanked my mother and my father and my other

mother and my other father, but when I
thanked them all I still
had fearfulness inside of me, mysterious.

As water conjures fire and fire, water, I discovered
that within I bore a boy who bore
my own name whom I had not thanked.

That night I dreamed of the field
of folk – the man with the fistful
of radishes, the passionate one, and the neighbor

whose granddaughter's eyes were closing for ever
and ever, and the hippie babysitter
with the white dog on the white leash, and

the CPA with the lemon Bonaventure. All seemed
to look on me with pity, as though
they knew my fate, knew its necessity.

I woke and there on the brilliant field outside
my window they were gathered,
a congregation circling the boy

I bore who bore my name, all staring
at the little flower on
the peach tree I had planted in my sleep.

Coda
(to a friend)

That convex mirror was a gift your drunkenness gave you, pried
from your elevator door one night. Elevators and small, elevator-like

restaurants, and the driver's seats of rented cars are where I picture
you. You take after your ancestors, butchers and last-makers, shaping

the slaughter behind culture, warp of laughter, woof of sadness.
You are an elegist at heart, but loss shocks you; your drawers are piled

with cuff-links and tie-clips somebody's uncle's uncle wore. The watch
you wear keeps ticking away, away, from the watch-shop where, deep

inside the last century, it caught your grandfather's eye. Even then it ticked
toward your wrist, toward this restaurant nearing closing time: the wine,

the underdone lamb. On 13th Street the present just got out; back home
the past (part theft, part gift) reflects close up how far away you seem.

Mechanical Wall, 1982
(on my birthday)

In school a wall kept the other half
      of the sixth-grade class mysterious
to us. Miss Rush would make it part
      on holidays, for awful parties where

we weren't allowed to flirt. When her echo,
      Miss Costello, shouted *Go* the wall slowly
withdrew into itself and we were face
      to face with kids who seemed that instant

artificial, blown from molten glass or molded
      in papier-mâché – not kids we knew already
anyway, from recess or from last year's class.
      It should have felt like we were staring

at ourselves, because we were; in one
      case, James Guillette beheld his twin
brother Marcel slowly revealed by
      the parting wall, and all of us knew the insides

of each other's houses, the divorces, mothers
      who sucked from bottles, sisters who got cancer or
who moved away to live in the trailers
      of older men who treated them like daughters.

We knew each other's lives by heart. Maybe
      that's why we looked so hard at one another
or why I peer at my own face today (same
      face as yesterday) in the mirror as

aghast sometimes I peer out our back window
      at unseasonable weather, snow in April, tight buds
this February on the cherry. Miss Rush
      was thirty, childlike, and unattractive.

She had once been a nun but now
      lived with a woman on the edge of town. We tried
to hurt her as best we could about it, but
      somehow she stayed nice. That pissed us off.

Self-Storage

Bring me your amateurish try
at taxidermy, fleur-de-lys

upholstered chair, flea-bitten oven mitt, replica Mars lander, old
         suit, bad

choice, wrong turn.
Bring me your freak, your odd, your ugly

rug, dull knife, dull life. Threatening noise heard
over and over in your skull, a bell

how many thousand decibels
loud, how much distraction, sadness, everything

is safe with me and out of sight.

                              *

America the widow
sorting through his drawer

of fisted socks. The ice shedding
itself inside the water glass.

The diagnosis. The dozen
childlike men begging for medication.

The monkey screaming behind
iron bars. Tender objects:

the dried corsage. America
a certain model

motorcycle, rare Beatles
butchered baby cover

safe, all safe,
all out of sight.

*

Are you the phone call
or the military

base, *North Carolina*
or *Vermont*, the rapist or my
aunt sent

far away for basic training,
senator
or sergeant, mother's tears

or father's stern
embarrassed
order to shut up? The den

or the phone, the voice
or the street noise, or television's

usual banal exuberance? America
they wanted

her to marry him.

*

Of all things seen
beside the highway I

am most like you. The stories
of lunatics and pack rats

storing old newspapers
broken bottles

63

scribbles animal remains
are true. Also

the corpses. Also
the stolen stereo.

A priest stores
jeweled chalices in me, no questions asked.

                             *

O pension everyone
agreed upon.

O slave, sieve, place
to put the precious useless things.

Aubade

I want to build but not
what I prayed
to build all the shrinking May nights, the lengthening

November nights, I want to build instead a bird's
body entirely
out of carpenter's right angles

and joinery, vices and saws, a lifelike bird!
I've made my own life
neat as a knot, tight as a fist –

strange how easily the ordinary becomes
ordinary, you and I
and the little vinyl modules we look back on

with regret or tenderness, and then
the strings and horns
and then the whole orchestra piles it on!

There's a nugget of what I want
to be in the statement
I am lonely most of the time, and tired of love.

It explains why I always get caught
in the bathroom making
my face make cruel expressions back at me.

But if I build for us a little bird
of pine and nails, we'll
hold the homemade, fidgety body in our hands

all dawn and, since we made it and
can prove it, even
its terror, even its fearful call, we'll call it ours.

Orange Tree

Dream of the bitter
greenish flesh of a tiny orange tree we grew

upstairs in our
bow window: I am eight or nine.

In life, I hoped
the flesh
would end up sweet

the way the fist-sized oranges in grocery bags turn

sweet, the way bought fruit does
almost always. But in my dream

I asked a man, my grandfather
but with the face
of an actor, playing him better

than he played himself, an actor

playing me
convincingly, a phony rented orange tree so real, the whole

set crafted by a new technique to look
just as I left it –
I asked

*

Sir, will you
cook these oranges?

Yes said the man, my grandfather, and led
me to an oven
where the green flesh of the orange tree turned orange

for me, sweet and edible, whatever

I could want.

*

I woke and spoke these words to you, since you
were nearest; and
you heard, since you were there.

NATURAL HISTORY

(2005)

I

He wanted to feel the same way over and over.

WALLACE STEVENS,
'This Solitude of Cataracts'

Love Song (Smelt)

When I say 'you' in my poems, I mean you.
I know it's weird: we barely met.
You must hear this all the time, being you.

That night we were at opposite ends of
the long table, after the pungent
Russian condiments, the carafes of tarragon vodka,

the chafing dishes full of boiled smelts
I was a little drunk: after you left,
I ate the last smelt off your dirty plate.

Love Song (Sycamores)

Stop there, stop now, come no closer,
I said, but you followed me anyway.
You made a bed for us in the woods.
There were sycamore boughs overhead.

Stop there. Stop now. I calculated that
the number of birds singing
on any given morning
was a function of the sycamores plus my hangover.

I said, *Stop there*, but you followed me
even when I tore our bed to pieces,
I did that, I brought anger into the bower
and the sycamores became menacing shoulders.

And the birds cried, scared, a little embarrassed.
And we paced back and forth, under
the menacing shoulders of the sycamores.
The birds made nests inside our heads.

When you held my fist between your two hands,
I pretended to be subdued. But then
I opened my fist easily
and scattered your strength all over the bower.

When you ran towards me, I said, *Stop there,*
stop now, you'll end up
in a stranger's life; and when you ran away
I said the same words over again, louder.

Pastoral

The woodpecker flew to the woodpile, pecked and fled.
The fox hid. The dog begged. The squirrel slept.
Nobody saw what the child did, silent, behind his book.

Out in the road, headlights were a hard metaphor,
everywhere passing, spot, spot: why do
the neighbors claim to 'adore all things Malaysian'?

You could date their house to another century,
give it an obsolete use, an obsolete industry,
say a lathe-making shop or a barn for threshing.

You could see the title on the child's book. But
what made the fox stay hid, the bird stay fled,
what held the sadness animal outdoors all night?

Poem Beginning with a Line from Frost

as if regret were in it and were sacred
     as if regret itself were a river and want

that was the source of the river flowed
     through the river, more and more the more

the river thickened towards the boring lake
     where what stirred once went terribly quiet.

This is indistinguishable from happiness.
     This standing water was a mindful current once.

Once was a mindful current: now leaden, still;
     it is ourselves we most resemble, now. Now

the maples that had been nowhere gather. When
     we look down what we look down on is our own.

Romance
(after *The Winter's Tale*)

I scorned you, and when you begged for mercy, I banished you.
Scorning, begging, banishing – that's what the script said.
My life was tragic, was the plot. Disaster sought me out.

Onstage, it was different. I packed your lunch;
I dropped you off, with a playful pat on the ass.
I made sure you saw me glance, once, in the rearview mirror

where I could see you showing me you saw me glance, once.
The night before, we'd partied on a rented tugboat
drifting down the narrow river: from the shore, smooth jazz

was heard between the surges of an ancient outboard motor.
Strangers on the shore guessed, correctly, someone had retired.
The microphone carried the tones, only the tones, of his

sentimental, endless *vale*. Then laughter, then more smooth jazz.
But now my radio told of a dire national emergency:
panic; folk forms of prophecy: omens, conspiracies.

Someone hung up the river, like a long dress on a hanger.
It touched the sky, then fell to the cement, as if the hanger
suddenly snapped. The radio was aghast and hysterical.

And so disaster happened offstage, to others. I was spared.
In Shakespeare when you are banished, time stops for you.
Years later, when you reappeared, you were my daughter's age.

Four Horaces

I *To Dan Chiasson Concerning Fortune*

Far out in the gray waters there are storms, there are crews
in trouble right now, as I write this, as you read this
letter or poem or whatever it is they drown, listen Dan,

the shoreline is no safe harbor either, its sharp rocks
rip even the stoutest hull like it's a wasp's nest
and the wasps swarm the shore, forget the shore, Dan;

oh and Dan, forget that big house inland, that house was built
with envy, not wood, not brick, not stone; it is hell
also to be under the tall tree when the storm rolls in,

leaves fill the air and eddy everywhere, there is no shelter
when the tower falls and the little city surrounding
cries 'Eek!' and they start unzipping body bags pronto.

Oh, love is a yo-yo: when you're high, you're already
feeling the pull of gravity, but when you're low,
it's really magical how you climb up the way you fell.

I've made my heart so calloused I can't be cheered,
but you know, Dan, I'm never lonely, and that's something.
In the winter, I don't shiver, I just sit there smiling.

In the summer, I never smile – I play cards indoors.
Apollo isn't always throwing darts, you know –
he has a lyre too and he likes to throw lyre parties.

It's sunny somewhere, Dan. The sun is shining somewhere.

The water at the bottom of the river, way down, the coldest
darkest water: if that water were your only drinking water
what would you do: thirst forever? Or drink the freezing water?

If A, send me a postcard from la-la land, where
Mom bays like a donkey and Dad is an oil slick,
because that's where dehydration takes you, fast.

If B, I'd buy the biggest wool parka I could find
and put it where the sun don't shine – otherwise
you'll feel a subzero chill no mug of tea will thaw.

I chose B, and now it's winter, and I'm outside your door
like a baby seal on an ice island, waiting
to be clubbed or saved by a Green New Zealander.

Come out. When Dan beats off again, when
he drifts away the way he always does, come out:
zip up that pantsuit and rescue me from my Horatian

sense of humor! There's a great jazz bar nearby
that doesn't charge a cover. They will play
only the nine jazz songs we know, over and over.

And the world will narrow the way it always does
when we're together, only nine jazz songs
ever written, and we know every one by heart.

And if some kid from the local jazz college walks in
and starts playing the tenth song, that's when
we get our clubs and club him like a baby seal.

III *After Party*

Helena, when you froth with the names of stars
I wonder is it a star's kiss, a star's trace
from last night's after party that perplexes me?

You can't buy the tears that adorn my eyes
on eBay or in the diamond district. Those
bruises on you aren't temporary henna tattoos.

Some star put them there after the after party,
before you made him taste the back of your throat.
I know what happens at those after parties, where

Absolut sponsors everything. Everyone puts a drop
of honey somewhere up inside their body and
the game is, where is it, who can find my honey drop?

Meanwhile, where is your Horace? Home, as usual,
translating Dan Chiasson's
petty agonies into his frantic, ancient Latin.

IV *Peeled Horse*

Helena, now that you have moved away
to a patrician county in New Jersey,
there's a horse under your ass, where I once was.

I would like to make that horse into
an anatomical drawing of himself, all
bone and tissue and staring eye sockets.

I've studied the masters: Battista Franco's
cabinets of femurs and knees, and
the banana-peel exposed skulls of Lucas Kilian –

how would you like to ride that peeled horse,
its bone saddle rattling all day, turning
your ass to bone in the New Jersey afternoon?

Tulip Tree

Out late and the night is a ruin, my voice says
the night is a ruin, my voice doesn't say a thing,
my poem says my voice doesn't say a thing,

your voice says my poem says my voice
doesn't say a thing. Your parents own the tulip tree
we lie under, but they don't own the night.

Nobody does, not even taxpayers! That's why
instead of overhearing a guitar or, from behind curtains,
watching people change, instead of telling stories

I 'obsess', as you say, about my tone of voice.
People change. Sometimes at night, curtains drawn,
they turn infinite upon each other, just for fun.

I want fried clams, the ones with gritty fat bellies.
If I strike the apocalyptic tone you like, won't you
drive up Route 1 with me, right now, to find those clams?

Made-up Myth

In the story of the bees, the lovers fall asleep
as flowers and wake as flesh, human flesh
stung so deep, so many times, it hurts the bone.

The way a wheel turns in space, in place,
over and over and gets nowhere –
with agony added, that's what the lovers feel.

Scholars translate the inscription above their bodies,
Beware – my body is spoiled meat, my spit
will parch you, it will never be your sweet milk.

They are made of such strange wishes. Once
he cupped a bee inside his bare palms
on a dare, and felt it slowly electrocute itself.

They are made of such strange dreams, bee-like dreams:
a peach orchard she never played in as a child,
where overnight the peaches never turned to stone.

Who slept as a wildflower, slept as a metaphor,
wakes to feel real pain, the scholars say,
even as the lovers writhe forever in myth-land.

Scholars, if they go down to the riverbank, under
the anchorage, you know the spot, if the lovers
lie down together there, will they wake as flowers?

Love Song (Toll)

It was near dawn. That night I'd
memorised Ralegh's poem
'Nature, That Washed Her Hands in Milk'.

Milk. Jelly. Light. Shit. Dust.
Time that doth not wash
his hands, time that is rust...

The bridges and the rivers
they spanned began
trying to begin to shine, as from within.

Near dawn. But when I thought
of all the possible bodies sleeping
in possible apartments, I got into my car

later or earlier than ever before,
later or earlier than ever before
paid the toll-taker my handful of glimmering change.

The road from here to there goes on forever.
Miles pass without a single
notable billboard. The toll-taker, smaller, smaller, vanishes.

I drove through dawn. Miles, then hundreds of miles,
passed, and still the same dull low-slung
sun, the moon behind a gunnysack curtain.

When I climbed into bed beside you it was
still dawn, and it is still dawn
now I've driven back home. You could be anyone.

II

Natural History

In Africa, I saw once with my own eyes a most amazing thing –
a bridegroom turn into a bride upon the altar.

> PLINY,
> *Natural History*, Book IV

The Eye is not satisfied with seeing,
nor the Ear filled with hearing.

> ECCLESIASTES 1:8

1 The Sun

There is one mind in all of us, one soul,
       who parches the soil in some nations

but in others hides perpetually behind a veil;
       he spills light everywhere, here he spilled

some on my tie, but it dried before dinner ended.
       He is in charge of darkness also, also

in charge of crime, in charge of the imagination.
       People fucking flick him off and on,

off and on, with their eyelids as they ascertain
       with their eyes their love's sincerity.

He makes the stars disappear, but he makes
       small stars everywhere, on the hoods of cars,

in the compound eyes of skyscrapers or in the eyes
       of sighing lovers bored with one another.

Onto the surface of the world he stamps
       all plants and animals. They are not gods

but he made us worshippers of every
       bramble toad, black chive, we find.

In Idaho there is a desert cricket that makes
       a clocklike tick-tick when he flies, but he

is not a god. The only god is the sun,
       our mind – master of all crickets and clocks.

II The Elephant

How to explain my heroic courtesy? I feel
    that my body was inflated by a mischievous boy.

Once I was the size of a falcon, the size of a lion,
    once I was not the elephant I find I am.

My pelt sags, and my master scolds me for a botched
    trick. I practiced it all night in my tent, so I was

somewhat sleepy. People connect me with sadness
    and, often, rationality. Randall Jarrell compared me

to Wallace Stevens, the American poet. I can see it
    in the lumbering tercets, but in my mind

I am more like Eliot, a man of Europe, a man
    of cultivation. Anyone so ceremonious suffers

breakdowns. I do not like the spectacular experiments
    with balance, the highwire act and cones.

We elephants are images of humility, as when we
    undertake our melancholy migrations to die.

Did you know, though, that elephants were taught
    to write the Greek alphabet with their hooves?

Worn out by suffering, we lie on our great backs,
    tossing grass up to heaven – as a distraction, not a prayer.

That's not humility you see on our long final journeys:
    it's procrastination. It hurts my heavy body to lie down.

III Purple Bush

The whiff of an extinguished candle
      will sometimes cause a miscarriage.

Eels must travel far upstream to where
      the river becomes a ribbon to spawn.

In that shallow water their babies risk
      exposure to the harsh midday sun.

Seeing a blind man in the ninth month
      can result in babies born without faces.

Their nurses use rare dyes to paint
      nearly permanent eyes and noses

on these featureless babies, but the use
      of such dyes causes sterility in women.

A sterile woman is a plague on armies.
      Whole armies have been slaughtered

for the barrenness of one soldier's wife.
      If the soldier lives, he's stoned to death or hanged.

Wade deep into the woods, go far from home,
      you will find a purple bush. The berries

of this bush bring perfect health, but health
      stirs envy, and envy makes the neighbor a killer.

IV The Hyenas

Picture a house in a storybook. It is some color
      houses never are – sky blue, or fire-engine red.

The winding trail that leads to its front door is
      crisscrossed by trees. But when you turn the page

the undulating hills around the little house
      begin to fill with voices. These voices cannot

be drawn. You must imagine the voices, because
      the little people in the storybook cannot hear;

they are cartoons. You thought you were an ignorant
      cartoon, but part of what these voices are saying

is that you are not, come out, come out. In some
      legends they know your name, and say it sweetly;

in others they coo like doves or whine like
      injured dogs. As you stare at the page, the house,

the trees, the voices grow louder, saying come out,
      come out; now they are everywhere, the way water

is everywhere when you are underwater.
      On the last page of the storybook the people

look sad, but it is not because the storybook
      is over. They live in there. It was a momentary

catastrophe. But you will never again live happily
      in your house, its acres and acres of silence.

V The Bear

In quiet, in the exquisite privacy of a cave, a bear
       gives birth. Outside the cave it's rain, a driving rain,

but inside there is no sound, only the thump-thump
       of her convulsing body and her babies' cries.

Her cubs are white screaming lumps, eyeless until
       she licks their eyes into place, bald until

she paints fur up and down their bodies with her tongue.
       It is a litter of five, at least; it is hard to see

how many have burrowed under her soft belly.
       Also, this is ancient Rome; it is hard to see through

so much time. It makes you wonder how many
       other beautiful sights are hidden away in time,

a cavelike element noted for its dimness. Now she
       and her cubs are emerging from the cave, leaving

one weakling behind. He is lame, and will not survive
       this rainy night two thousand years ago. By now

he is vanishing into the floor of the dark cave,
       even his newly painted fur, even his fresh eyes.

By now he's gone entirely from view.
       All the caves on this hill are identical again.

VI From the Life of Gorky

Thinking of the local murdered girl, the news, her hose, and the word 'holler' (*She hollered*, said the dishwasher who'd been released, of course, earlier that summer), I read the first chapter of Gorky's *My Childhood*.

*

Gorky's father's corpse is on the kitchen floor, his mother combing her husband's hair, when suddenly she hollers *Jesus!*, writhing on the cold floor there, beside the body.

*

What happens next, you won't believe – she gives birth, propped up against her husband's corpse, right there in chapter one of Gorky's memoir.

*

Gorky's little brother hollers his first cries.

*

It's gotten late.

*

I'm reading in the dark.

VII Georgic

Whether to twine the flowers around the maples, whether
    the chipped antler found in the sod portend a hot summer,

whether a hot summer portend interiors fogged by breath,
    reeking of sweat and shit, and can the hoe save us,

and can the spade, and if we pot the peach pit
    in a terracotta pot, will we have peaches next year?

Will we have peaches ever? If the clouds overhead
    spell *Angie and Ed*, have we seen something spectacular?

Is there a pilot somewhere with an agile plane who'll write
    what we say in the sky? *I wish I were a tree*, wrote Herbert,

for sure then I should come to fruit or shade – what use,
    the pulse that makes the poem race weakens me, *what use*,

I found a shriveled cherry and a shrimp tail in my
    suit pocket, I never wear it, it hangs in the closet.

My forehead is blank like the sky and good for writing.
    Sparrow, make your nest in me, come down from the sky.

VIII Pliny

I stepped on a bird this morning. It had fallen between
      two parked cars. My boot heel made it make a quiet,

sobbing noise, not at all like birdsong. It was
      brittle and soft at once, like matchsticks inside

chewing gum. As a child in Rome, I dreamed someday
      I would be Emerson's 'transparent eyeball'. I tried

different ways to disappear: I wore a football helmet
      everywhere. What I found out was: you can't

be a transparent eyeball in a football helmet.
      I feel better in the dark. I compare the dark

to chocolate: some rich, naughty substance covering
      my body. That would be invisible – to be dipped in chocolate.

That's no football helmet. What if pain turned
      the bird inside out, what if its own scale were volcanic?

You've got to get yourself dirty to imagine it.
      You've got to get down on all fours and bark.

IX From the Life of Gorky (II)

I am on a hill near Nizhniy. The time is dawn. It is 1880.

That outline is a constable.

That is his splattering boots.

We're here to bury my father: why else would those spades be stuck in a loam pile?

Now he blows a whistle, shouts, *Hurry up!*

The wind dies, and the weeping increases.

*

We're in a time of incessant action, up/down up/down. The pile shrinks as the sun rises.

*

Now it is morning in New York City, and I've made a gross discovery: my kosher salt is full of something's larvae.

Why would you lay your eggs in salt? Can anyone tell me, what kind of creature leaves its babies behind in a box of salt?

*

Now it is morning over Nizhniy.

*

My father's canary-yellow coffin is already a memory.

X The Elephant (II)

The others were baited with serene, contented elephants,
 brought indoors for the first time ever, given

barley juice and honey poured from the skull of a monkey
 But what they did to me – it fills me with weird shame.

It's worse than when I got drunk at the department party
 and showed off that photograph of my anus. Worse than

when I was caught masturbating at the Laundromat.
 In Ethiopia, you see, I'm all the meat there is. He waited

in the bole of the tree, keeping a lookout for me,
 the only laggard. I read that Stevens was like me,

a slow, methodical walker. It is left to later generations
 to draw the line where daydream, revery, etc., end and

'great poetry' begins. He rode atop my right haunch,
 holding on to my tail. When his ax struck, it was

so warm at first, I thought I'd pissed my pants.
 I had not pissed my pants. I had a mouthful of dirt.

XI Making Purple

Nibble what nibbles you, play dead, play bored;
      play sad, shell gaping, like the cockle used for bait;

like the melting purple eat the mud, be seen through
      like the pebble purple, soft like the reef purple.

Imagine yourself suffusing a woman's gown or sheets
      your bloodstream running through her inkwell.

Those rich dyes once were your ideas, your love
      of broccoli rabe. Half-killed cockles attract purples,

the reef is littered with open mouths waiting to snap.
      I am trying to make my pain attractive, my yearning

pretty. A man caught me in a fine-ply lobster pot.
      He scalded me until I nearly died, then threw me back.

I gape like this, because of the ordeal. Did you foresee
      this moment, where what you intended to devour

devours you? Did you know they'd haul us up
      into the suffocating air, our bodies fused together?

XII Pliny (II)

I became a tiny eye to see into the eye of a sparrow,
        a cricket's eye, a baby's eye; when I looked

at the night sky, I made my eye as big as history, for
        the night sky is a kaleidoscope of past times,

as noted astronomer Carl Sagan said. I watched TV and
        made my eye a TV: lidless, rash gazer at whatever happens,

casting shadows of what happens for the neighbors,
        whose eyes are the size of windows, my windows, and sharpen

their sight to voluptuous desire, voyeur voyeur
        pants on fire. Anything half-seen becomes what's on,

becomes the neighbors' newscast, lotto drawing, rerun.
        How do you know a child has died except by watching

trays of casseroles brought in, the old sit-down,
        peoples' bodies doing as bodies will against the wall?

XIII Inscribed on a Lintel

I was born beside a quarry. I played in granite
      spray and gravel, dust up to my elbows.

I was born beside the ocean, I played in the tide,
      at night I sucked my arm to get the salt out.

I was born beside a mountain, I played under
      evergreens. At night my life seemed haunted.

I lived beside a quarry, I worked deep in the earth,
      I made my body a drill to burrow into stone.

I lived beside the ocean, I worked inside the water,
      I made my body a net and I cast myself wide.

I lived beside a mountain, I worked inside the wood,
      I made my body a saw and I cleared a field.

All my life when I worked, I disappeared inside
      my work; so when my work ended, I disappeared.

XIV News

The news on the forgotten friend is not good, no
      not at all: his head is swelling up, but inside,

where there's no room left. Outside, America is empty –
      spilled towns, old industries, territories spiky

with wildflowers, the sky is a pile of air, even
      the ocean is a possible frontier, and still his head

decides to grow in the wrong direction. It changes
      colors as you drive west, O it goes green to

brown, brown to red, red to green, and the West
      is just like the movies, cacti flower there.

Would you ever drive across America for a friend,
      would you watch canyons pass, plains, mountains

pass, would you drive that far for any reason
      but to see a girl, preferably a near stranger?

XV Randall Jarrell

I've never written in a way that really pleases Dan.
    His opinion is invaluable to me, but I am shy –

so shy I left the earth five years or so before
    he arrived. He likes '90 North', I know –

and the Rilke poem whose title he can't presently recall.
    I did that one with him in mind. A corpse is stiff,

its arms extended like a man giving 'commandments'.
    Of course the dead do command us, in their way.

For example: reread my last book, *The Lost World*.
    Now compare my boyhood in L.A. to Dan's:

read his first book, *The Afterlife of Objects*.
    He tried on the confessional style for a while.

If people hurt you, tell on them: perhaps you'll heal.
    If language hurts you, make the damage real.

What else? A poem about a hopping toad should never be
    an allegory for epistemology or Wittgenstein.

Read Proust for soft focus. Read Rilke for nostalgia.
    Richard Wilbur was the future once, but weren't we all?

XVI The Pigeon

Once startled, you shall feel hours of weird sadness
        afterwards. This is known as the rule of the pigeon.

This is the rule of the Herbert scholar: your head
        shall come to rest in a Ziploc terrarium, not a park.

You shall be fêted in the pages of *New York* magazine,
        and at department meetings, over eggnog, mourned.

This is the rule of the girl you loved: you shall heave
        and heave all night, alone, and not from love, not

from anything like love. Peel that mattress off your back,
        but peel you never will the remorse-stain, and

this is the rule of The Who, you shall be Muzak,
        you shall be orchestral, electronic and franchised.

You shall be blood, is the rule of the sleepless night,
        and you shall be drained of blood, is the rule of dawn.

The scholar and the pigeon shall inhabit the same street,
        your street, but you shall remember the pigeon longer.

XVII The Elephant (III)

When he hit me square on the head I said *Better to die*
　　this way than in obscurity, on the empty plain.

A heron and a hawk, a monkey carrying a monkey skull,
　　a lion on fire and a pack of eyeless wolves

were what I feared, my rib cage rocking to and fro
　　in the sun, in the wind, all day and night, a dinghy

anchored in rough seas. Not this: my body a sack of
　　garbage, hooves bound, the world turned upside down.

This is a beautiful country, said John Brown on his way
　　to the gallows, *I have not cast my eyes o'er it before –*

that is, in this direction. And I said, *What a beautiful banquet,*
　　I am honored to contribute. They cleaned my skull

with pulverised mica for their cornucopia: those were
　　my eye sockets overflowing with black grapes, herrings

lying in piles of their own, jewel-like, dewlike roe
　　made the crown of my head, and the bride was beautiful.

XVIII 'There Is a Star in the Sea'

(Pliny, *Natural History*, Book IX)

'There is a star in the sea, and it burns up everything
        it touches. Though men who walk on land deny it,

one night a star fell from the sky and landed in the sea.
        It had the good sense to become a fish, but the wit

to keep its shape. It sleeps on the bottom of the sea,
        but one day I'll play a trick on it – I'll turn the ocean

upside down! Then it will shine again, coral bluff,
        rusted galleon in the night sky, and I will pray to it.'

XIX Georgic (II)

The flowers that fade, the flowers that don't, the wax
        begonias made to look like real ones by an artisan in

Quebec, the wax insects that buzz nearby and the wax fragrance
        that attracts them, the wax lovers walking idly, their

wax promises, the entire scene done in a shoe box with a peephole
        to grant the wax lovers privacy, making your looking,

your mere looking, forbidden and therefore wonderful –
        what was that again, listen – this wax man and woman,

what disappointment is it now bows him down, as she
        half-comforts him, while her other half makes a call

on a cell phone? The flowers beam anyway, clueless.
        They ignore us – if what I mean by 'us' is the wax lovers,

you and I, making a fetish of our privacy again, putting joy
        in someone's eye. And that's what I mean by us.

XX Things I Saw with My Own Eyes

I saw a stout man turn into a bird, then shed
      his feathers, one by one, and become a woman.

I saw a hippocentaur preserved in honey, wheeled
      through town by a bellowing entrepreneur.

On a feast day, a man lay down upon the banquet
      and spewed forth sweet wine from his genitals.

It soaked everyone's clothes and stained our skin –
      hilarity ensued, until the wine turned to blood.

When we were soaked with his blood, the man died.
      There was chaos in the hall, and much howling.

Tribes in India howl when they are happy. I saw
      a woman give birth to a hundred children,

like drops from a dripping faucet or luggage on
      a luggage carousel. If you are perfectly still

and you lie down in a field, soon your body
      will be covered by sparrows, but move an inch

and they fly away all at once, leaving you naked,
      and scatter everywhere above you in the sky.

XXI From the Life of Gorky (III)

On the boat I ate watermelons and cantaloupe in secret. There was a man on board, forever drunk, dressed like a policeman, who forbade the eating of fruit. If you got caught with fruit, he scolded you and threw it in the river. This he called his 'wild justice'.

*

Was it justice when, one night, approaching shore, he threw himself overboard?

*

More vodka for Grandmother. Another of her saint-devoured-by-a-wild-beast stories.

*

In a corner of the cabin, wrapped in a white sheet tied with a bright red ribbon, my newborn brother Maxim – who caught death, Mother said, from his father's dead hand.

*

A storm. Rainwater whips the horse's eye of the porthole I look out from.

*

When my uncle said, *Alexei, why do you cry?* I answered, *For Maxim: the storm tosses him to and fro.*

XXII The Burial of Children

Children buried in pairs, twins buried in a single coffin,
    their arms entwined, or wrapped in one white sheet;

children buried with curios and whatnots, pictures
    of themselves as infants, their pets killed and buried

beside them; lacquered with honey, with lemonade,
    spearmint children, lavender and thyme children,

a goldenrod crown for the golden boy, wheat and whey
    and cornstalks for the farmer's girl, and some children

were buried in large glass jars. Fucking fly laid its eggs
    in my box of salt, and a girl I know misplaced her baby,

now every baby she sees she thinks it's hers. Children
    were buried in large glass jars, bent fetus-like

at the neck at the waist at the knees at the toes as though
    the glass were that sweet fluid they first breathed.

Be careful what you love, what you presume to love.
    Who suckles salt, with the sticky honey jar nearby?

XXIII Which Species on Earth Is Saddest?

When we wake up in our bodies, first we weep.
        We weep because the air is thick as honey.

Even the air is a body. Ours is the bottommost
        and newest body, nested inside other, older ones

(though the mother's body is repairing itself now;
        there's no trace of us anywhere on her;

why are we part of every body but our mother's?)
        Die as soon as possible, the Scriptures say.

And many do – or soon enough, as in the tales of
        a swollen boy, now years ago, in farthest Africa,

who filled a grove of cherry trees with tears, then
        vanished into the grove. He hides behind trees.

That's death for you, a fragrant grove to hide within,
        your sister looking for you in a pile of cocaine.

That's weeping for you. Grief is a cherry grove.
        Don't be born at all. My friend is on fast-forward now

to reach the scene where they erase her childlessness.
        She knows she hid that kid somewhere inside of her,

but where? We know nothing else except by learning:
        not walking, not eating. Only to cry comes naturally.

XXIV The Soil

Stay whole, stay full, stay mild: the soil absorbs
      whatever falls: apple, animal, apple-pie wrapper.

Anywhere on earth you go, get yourself full on
      other people's mothers, other people's sweethearts.

Drought come, flood you with new food. Cancer riff,
      cancer chafe and giggle, soil stay full.

Upholstery swallow you, you stay full. Roast
      destroy your muscle, you stay mild. Wall-to-wall

cover you, you stay whole: you're wall-to-wall on earth.
      My mother ached for weeks, then blossomed into

a pain petunia. The president's head wound is on rewind.
      Over and over the skyscraper zips and unzips.

Now I am famous in the world of arts and letters
      many Internet entries are me, many are not –

there's my name on the official embalmers' site, but
      that's not me answering the Q&A. Someday

I will be the Q&A on the embalmers' site, but
      if the arithmetic holds, I'll beat the embalmer.

The sweetheart and the mother disappear, but
      everybody here is present and accounted for.

My girl malignant cries that she used to be benign;
      my neighbor wheelchair was a volleyball champion.

Stay whole, stay full, stay mild: the world is a cradle –
      no, a wheelbarrow. It hauls shit and dirt and hay.

III

It is known that one elephant, who was rather slow in learning his tricks and had been punished severely by his master's beating, was discovered later that night, alone in his tent, practicing those tricks.

PLINY,
Natural History, Book VIII

'Scared by the Smallest Shriek of a Pig, and When Wounded, Always Give Ground.'

What we saw on festival day: play infantries
with real spears, real veins, a real soldier
pulled across the festival grounds trailing blood
the way a paintbrush is pulled across a canvas;
lesser mischief, on the periphery: my friend saw
a man gouge out an elephant's eyes with a shovel,
and the elephant cried, *Oh, Murder, I am Murdered!*
the way we do – wordless, comical, like a choir of kazoos:

is that poetry? Or is poetry picking the scarcest word,
say, 'charred' instead of 'burned' –
as in 'charred in a fire'? Real life is so raw,
all on its own; it hurts; words should perhaps
protect us from real life.
Perhaps words should be a shield, rather than
a mirror; and maybe poems should be
an ornamented shield, like the shields

gods made for their favorite soldiers,
sons and lovers. Poems should be
like people's faces by firelight:
a little true, for verification's sake,
but primarily beautiful. Or like
pomegranates: hard to open at first
but, when you get them open, full of sweet granules
of meaning. Once, when I was bathed in wine

as part of a military victory parade,
I was purple for a month –
I liked the looks of me that way,
like a giant pomegranate seed!
That's what a poem should be:
recognisable reality, but dyed,
a sign that someone here felt joy,
someone was released from pain,

one minute he lived he felt no pain,
the war was over, killing was over
and he was not killed, not maimed.
I liked myself that way. I remember
as a boy, after she had done her obsequies
to the moon, down at the riverbank,
my mother put me to bed and whispered,
'Frederick' – for that is my name – 'Frederick,

you saved my life; Mommy wanted to die
before she felt you stir inside her.'
It made me feel wonderful. Thereafter,
I never felt anything other
than completely central to her life –
what a gift that was. I suppose I understand
my future years in light of our intense
bond, my hours waiting for her outside

the dispatcher's office, the time she
dated a guy with a criminal record
and soon she found out why – I held her
that time, that time she was the calf
and I the mommy. She was a kind of guitar
to learn forgiveness on, its harmonies
and, yes, even its bungled chords.
And I learned to pity the powerful –

my trainer, forcing me to puff a cigarette,
was himself forced, by powers
far greater than he, to force me;
so I did it, though my lungs hurt,
though my lungs felt sandpapered after.
I almost wrote 'sadpapered' there; isn't it weird
the way the mind works, because
as I fill this paper up with words

I do feel sad, thinking of him lighting
that cigarette, placing it between my lips,
the wild applause, our strange
intimacy, and my relief – my God,
I thought I might swallow
that fire and become fire. Let me tell
you about my sister, Sarah, and a custom
that's long since been lost: Sarah

was hired to be a lying-in girl
by the Bridgeport Circus. This was before
the war, or rather, between them.
The ringmaster, not yet famous, invented
a new highwire act: a large bull
would carry a petite cow across
the wire, holding her in a bonnet
hung upon his trunk, the cow lying

in a pile of down blankets, moaning.
The crowd was stunned: never
had they seen an elephant carry
another elephant across the sky,
across the almost invisible single thread
of twine. Once the bull crossed
and backed down the ladder, though –
surprise! From the bonnet, a pair of calves

appear and sport around the ring!
'Lying-in Sarah' made the circus rich.
The ultimate fate of that circus need not
here be discussed: that fire was
a tragedy, just let me say; and say also,
it was *not* Mother's fault. Sarah's
memorabilia are strewn all over
my apartment; someday I'll frame it all;

someday the world will know
her name and perhaps associate me
with her in some small way. I am aware
that in certain uncivilised places,
where men grunt at one another
and know not speech, know not poetry
or any other art that ennobles us,
elephants still are hunted for their tusks;

myself, I had my own removed as soon
as I had the money, and hired
an artisan to carve from them my life's story –
there is an icon of the moon; a river
icon; three figures together, representing
Sarah, my mother and me; a flag
to show my love of country…
but I've gone on too long. And plus,

the things people accumulate and say
'This was my life' – it isn't just boring,
it's also vaguely creepy, even if it was
once part of their bodies. Is it this way
with poetry? I hope not, since all day long
I write my poetry, my 'sadpaper'.
Let others say if I'm bronze or not, say
if this Frederick be a poet or a scribbler.

NEW POEMS

(2006)

Roman Song

Shit is the taste you want in your mouth,
said love, said love, *be a dog*,
I lost my heart in the gutter, in the filth,
carry it back to me in your teeth.

Love said *be a dog*, find the butcher
and the gutter, the run-off,
the blood stream flooding the sewer:
the water that sickens quenches desire.

Nothing breathing escapes your appetite.
Nothing to drink is an alien thirst.
Put everything living down your throat.
Your belly is vast as the world tonight.

Ignore your master's leash. Let food
be your master. Let everything
be food. Let everything taste good.
Let everything you eat be your good food.

A Posy

The cocklebur and ergot, horse chestnut, fescue taste not,
neither taste the green false hellebore nor jimsonweed
nor larkspur, nor even the wild black cherry, pigweed,
pokeweed, lupine and easter lily; regarding the cherry
there is a story, there is a story regarding the fescue,
men tell a tale about the green false hellebore, there are
accounts of the cherry, pokeweed, the Jack-in-the-Pulpit:
taste not, lest your skin harden, tingling like cooled wax;
lest your muscles straighten and snap like a candle
taste not the red oak lest your eyes redden and swell –

if you are hungry in this world you are in grave peril,
if it is food you want in this world beware, take care
never to go hungry so that the cocklebur or ergot say
jimsonweed pokeweed say *I am bread* lupine say *I am bread*

Mosaic of a Hare, Corinium, 100 AD

The boats pulling in, the boats pulling out, the top-hat
commerce of the 'infant century', crowds, crowds,
'the pulling and hauling' of street-life, the bomb
that filled the air with horse-hair and the ambulance after:

why wouldn't I hide in my little glass body? I have a clover-sprig
made of glass to aspire to, with my glass appetite.
I raise certain questions about art and its relation to stasis,
yet I despise the formalists as naïve and ahistorical.

Here's my problem with America: this "would be" that obliterates
all other moods, playing over and over in people's heads,
the abstract optative that destiny works out.
I don't have the luxury to think in terms of destiny.

What nobody seems to get about me is, though you're made of glass
it doesn't mean you don't have appetites: I do. Or fears: I do.
The day the darkness took the whole Basilica, I was afraid;
and equally afraid the day, centuries later, they switched the lights on.

Let rabbits think in terms of destiny: Whitman, the great
American rabbit poet, the rabbits in the government,
the rabbits that light and the ones that snuff out the fuse,
and all their pretty rabbit children, waiting to be casserole.

Aquarium

I am full of secrets, but none of them is yours.
You can't confide in the outside world.
The surface of the glass is your only conceivable body.

These traces of movement, sudden shadows, they're not fish.
There are varieties of life unknown to you.
Their whole identity is: you can't find out.

You can't find out, however hard you try, no matter
what you say, however "advanced" you are:
they swim away, these things that are not fish.

Look at those bodies on the street. Do you see
how beautifully designed the human body is?
How can you compare your mere column for containing water?

My mind contains everything except for fish.
The rumor of depth is your new atmosphere.
You can't confide in me. I'm not an aquarium.

You don't even rule your own body. Look at you,
Lost in this and that,

Here Follows an Account of the Nature of Birds

Here Follows an Account of the Nature of Fish.
Here follows a description of an unknown town.
Here follows the phoenix-flight from human eyes.
Here follow the friendship fish and langouste.
All the marvels of erotic danger follow here.
Here follows the phone number of a dead person.
Here follows a game based on perfect information.
Five minutes have passed since I wrote this line.
I mistook my baby's cry for the radiator hiss.
Here follows the address of a place to buy cocaine.
Big sadness come your way, sunrise, skyline.
Let's do it some new way next time we try.
Do you have anything you can put inside me?
Here Follows an Account of the Nature of Birds.

Little Boy

For a quarter you get a mess, for a half you get to make a mess,
for three-quarters you see somebody else's idea of god.
For one and a half anyone in that bar will marry you, marry you.
The daughter of the ruling class will piss upon your palm.
Her horse is America and you have your certain, broken destiny.

For a quarter somebody shows up with a briefcase, baggy baggy.
Everybody salivates and rifles though his wallet.
Then the bowed heads are like cattle through the wire fence feeding.
Then the heads thrown back, we feel love for our mothers.
Then the hard hands of our fathers are washed clean of dirt.

There is a cloud, there is, I could take you there now, I could.
Do you want to see this really amazing place with me?
There the bumblebee is free of the robber.
Here the robber roams, hungry, in the neon dawn;
there, after a little catnap, we snip old magazine ads.

Magazine

Let him kiss me with the kisses of water, for I am fire.
Let him kiss me with the kisses he keeps
behind his guitar, in the feverpitch garage loft.
Let him kiss me with the kisses of his brother's marijuana.

Then by the woodpile he instructed me in privacy,
privacy that makes the world go round,
privacy that men seek, sometimes by force, that women
let happen inside their skinny, stinging bodies.

Privacy was a glossy waterlogged magazine, and
the steady rain made a hard canopy on all sides;
and he did bestow upon me a high from the 10cc album jacket;
and his eyes were the eyes of a doe, white as cream, even in the middle.

Inside mom has strawberry soup on the woodstove, waiting.
She has to make it boil first before it starts to cool.
You can arrange nearly anything with the big boy next door.
And the three of us, once the soup cooled, supped.

Etruscan Song

No love like mine; no love; no love like mine
transformed a hotel room into a womb
and a womb into the child's cry;
no love, no love, no love like mine.

Read in the dark, one hand on cock
Etruscan lore in my Etruscan book –
justice had another flavor there,
buried the son to punish the father.

Drove bolt-fast down the Merritt Parkway
one night, alone, singing *Please Bury Me*;
drove up the following afternoon
with a spade saying *dig me up, someone*;

dug up, found the sun so hot it burned;
craved the chocolate cool of dirt,
the pupa-life underground,
the coffin-dark of a dirt coffin.

So made, no love like mine, a boy;
turned dirt from chocolate to clay;
the clay became, one day, a cry,
and the cry turned night to day.

Lincoln's Dream

It is impossible to state just how in love I am
with my own body, the white snows of me,
the sudden involutions and crevasses of me,
my muscles tensed in anger or fear or to fuck.

This is why, wherever I am, I am in Lincoln's dream.
A sentry stands by, the stairway is eerily lit,
light is a little milk-stain on people's faces,
the faces of my cabinet, grotesque and funny masks.

Who is dead in the White House? I demand. *Who's not?*
answers a soldier, pointing to a shrouded head
on my own body, encased like a gangly insect
on the catafalque, and the loud wails wake me up.

Reader, when you caress yourself in the morning,
amazed that you are made the way you are,
sure that yours is the finest body of all,
remember, you are Lincoln having Lincoln's dream.

NOTES

THE AFTERLIFE OF OBJECTS

'The Sensible Present Has Duration' (18): The title is taken from William James's *The Principles of Psychology*.

Self (28): Woodcutters in the Ganges delta wear wooden masks on the backs of their heads to confuse Bengal tigers, who only attack from the back. The poem is indebted to Elisa New's *The Line's Eye: Poetic Experience, American Sight*.

Boston (21): The phrase in quotes is from Henry James's *The American Scene*.

Cicada (40): The Greek adjective describing the cicada's song, *leirios*, is often translated 'lily-like'. The poem's source is the myth of the cicadas in Plato's *Phaedrus*.

NATURAL HISTORY

My title refers to Pliny the Elder's *Historia Naturalis*, which I first encountered after reading Italo Calvino's essay on it, 'Man, the Sky, and the Elephant'. The poems in the title-sequence and the longer poem that closes the book derive elements in their stance, their voice, and their cadence from Pliny. In a very few cases, as in 'The Elephant (I)', I have borrowed images and phrases from Pliny as well.

The lines attributed to John Brown in 'The Elephant (III)' were brought to my attention by Forrest Gander's book *Tom Awake*, where they serve as an epigraph. The poems about Gorky borrow ideas from Maxim Gorky's *My Childhood*. The line from Frost that opens 'Poem Beginning with a Line from Frost' is from 'West-Running Brook', and was suggested to me by Desales Hamson. The Horaces in Section I are composites of things I found in the odes of Horace and things I made up. These poems are indebted to David Ferry, whose translations of Horace formed totally my imagination of the Roman poet.